MW01408941

BRUNO'S BEST BIRTHDAY

Written by Megan Deliberto
Illustrated by Tiemoko Sylla

Enjoy!
Megan Deliberto

RODNEY K PRESS

Bruno's Best Birthday

Copyright ©2023 Megan Deliberto

All rights reserved. No part of this publication may be reproduced, distributed, or transmitted in any form or by any means, including photocopying, recording, or other electronic or mechanical methods, without the prior written permission of the publisher, except in case of brief quotations embodied in critical reviews and certain other noncommercial uses permitted by copyright law.

ISBN: 978-1-960111-06-7
Library of Congress:

Names, characters, and places are products of the author's imagination.
Front cover image, illustrations, and book design by Tiemoko Sylla.
First printing edition 2023.

Published by Rodney K Press
rodneykpress.com

To Sophia, Donovan, Dylan & Grayson
for helping inspire this story.
I will always love you.
I will always support you.

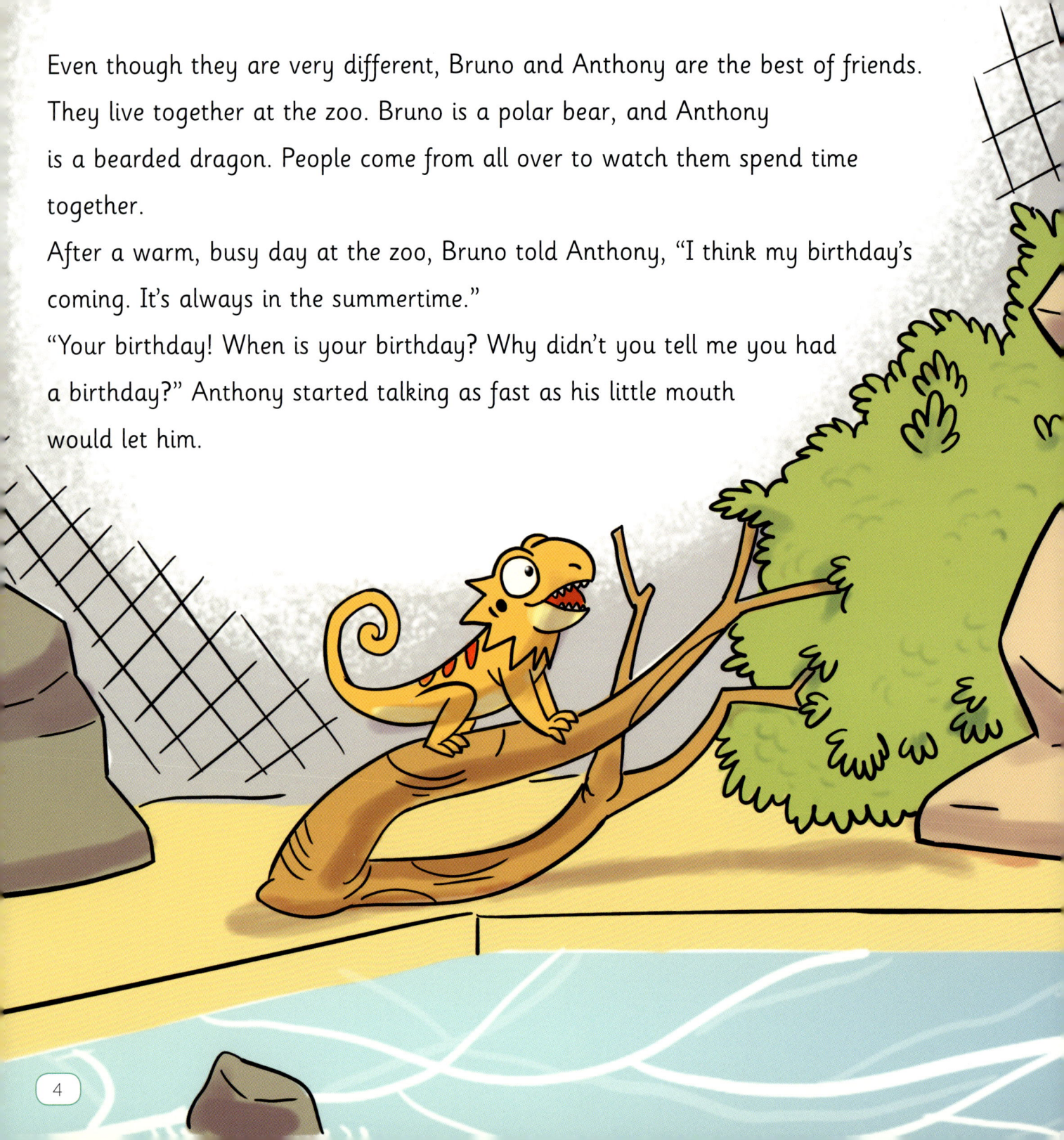

Even though they are very different, Bruno and Anthony are the best of friends. They live together at the zoo. Bruno is a polar bear, and Anthony is a bearded dragon. People come from all over to watch them spend time together.

After a warm, busy day at the zoo, Bruno told Anthony, "I think my birthday's coming. It's always in the summertime."

"Your birthday! When is your birthday? Why didn't you tell me you had a birthday?" Anthony started talking as fast as his little mouth would let him.

"Whoa, slow down little lizard," Bruno responded. "Of course, I have a birthday. Everyone has a birthday. Mine is June 13th. On that day, the zookeepers will bring me giant ice cubes and they'll put a birthday sign on the glass."

"What? No. A sign on the glass isn't enough! What about friends? Where are all the presents and treats?" Anthony asked impatiently.

"You forgot about the giant ice cubes. That's a special treat and a gift all rolled into one."

Anthony did not think ice cubes were enough either. Bruno deserved a birthday celebration as big as he was. "June 13th is in just a few days! We should have a party and invite our friends from around the zoo!!"

Bruno shook his furry head no. "You know I can't leave my habitat, and you're the only one that has ever found a way in. Besides, those are your friends. I've never been able to meet any of them. I'll have you this year, and that's enough for me."

That night, while Bruno was snoring giant polar bear snores, Anthony thought about his friend's birthday. He knew there had to be a way to make Bruno's birthday special. Before morning, Anthony had a plan to make this the best birthday for Bruno. Before coming to live with him, Anthony had visited many animals at the zoo. He had made some friends and thought they might be able to help throw Bruno a party.

Anthony snuck out of the polar bear den to find Sophia. She was a young giraffe and he found her munching on some leaves. She was already 10-feet tall, and she wasn't done growing. "Good morning Sophia!" Anthony yelled from far below. Sophia looked down and smiled at Anthony with a mouthful of leaves. She finished swallowing her meal before answering.

"Hey, little guy! What's going on?"

"My friend Bruno's birthday is coming up. Do you want to come to his party?" Anthony yelled back.

"Bruno's the polar bear, right? That sounds like a lot of fun. I've never been to a polar bear's party before, but my legs aren't long enough to get over the fences. What if I give you a gift for him instead?"

"That's a great idea!" Anthony responded happily. He watched as Sophia grabbed a pretty branch from a nearby tree. It was covered in small flowers and large green leaves. She yanked it clean off the tree and dropped it next to Anthony.

Anthony thanked her and dragged the branch back near Bruno's home. He hid it behind a shed where the zookeepers worked. He slipped back down the wall before Bruno was even awake for the day.

Early the next morning, Anthony went to see Dylan. He's a bottlenose dolphin and is a huge hit at the zoo. The guests love to watch him dance through the water and cheer when he would leap out of the pool.

"Dylan!" Anthony yelled. He had to yell to get Dylan's attention because it was hard to hear underwater.

"What's up little dude?" Dylan answered.

"I am throwing a birthday party for Bruno. Is there a way you can make it to the polar bear enclosure?"

"A party would be really cool, but unless I can swim from here to there, I'm stuck in my pool."

Before Dylan swam away, Anthony yelled out, "Sophia gave me a gift to give him. Do you want to give him something too?"

"Let me think...how about my hula hoop? I love to jump through it."

Anthony thought about this. A hula hoop was going to be hard to drag back, but a ball would roll much easier. "How about your basketball instead? That way I can roll it back."

"Right on, my bearded bud! I have plenty of extra basketballs floating around," Dylan said before he dove deep into the pool.

Anthony watched as Dylan shot up from the bottom and hit the basketball out of the water to where he was waiting.

After hiding the ball, Anthony ran over to see if Grayson, the African Elephant, might be able to come to the party. Grayson is so large that you can feel the ground rumble when he runs. He has giant floppy ears and the coolest trunk. He can pick up everything with that trunk.

Grayson ambled over to the fence where Anthony was waiting and, with a big yawn, asked, "Why are you here so early?"

"Want to come to Bruno's birthday party?" Anthony asked, hoping Grayson would have some way to leave the elephant enclosure.

"Do you know how mad my grandma would be if I tried to leave the herd? She is already mad that I am talking to you. She still thinks you are a mouse," Grayson grumbled.

"It's okay. So far, no one else can come either. I can bring him a gift from you though if you want."

"What do you give a polar bear for his birthday?" Grayson tapped his head with his trunk like he was trying hard to think of something. "I know!" Grayson cheered as he ran off toward his herd. A minute later, he came back holding his trunk in the air like it was filled with water.

"Don't squirt me!" Anthony squeaked as he hid behind a fence post. The last time Grayson shot water at him, it nearly washed him into a sewer drain.

"Calm down! I won't squirt you!" Grayson laughed as he placed a trunkful of peanuts on the ground next to Anthony.

"Oh, peanuts! These will be a fun treat for Bruno!" Anthony was able to put one peanut in his mouth and push the others with his head back to the shed.

The next morning, Anthony headed straight for the monkey house to visit Donovan. He is a black and white spider monkey who loves to climb and collect treasures that people drop into his exhibit.

"Hey Donovan, it's Bruno's birthday tomorrow. I'm throwing him a party!" Anthony called from the bridge next to Donovan's favorite tree.

"Can I come to the party?" Donovan loved parties.

"Yes! Can you come to our house?" If anyone could figure out how to make it over the high walls without Anthony's claws, it would be Donovan.

"Nah, my mom would get mad at me. The last time I tried to sneak out, she took away my toys for a week! But I have something I wanted to give Bruno anyway, and now it can be for his birthday! Stay here!"

Donovan swung away and scurried down the tree so fast it made Anthony dizzy. Before he knew it, Donovan was back holding a giant pair of red sunglasses. They were bigger than Anthony's entire body.

"Where did those come from?" Anthony laughed. The glasses were one of the most wonderfully ridiculous things he had ever seen.

"There was a birthday party here and there was a person with giant shoes and a crazy polka dot outfit. He dropped these over the wall by accident. Aren't they the coolest? I bet they'll fit Bruno!"

Anthony really wanted Bruno to have these sunglasses, but he had no clue how he would get them back to the shed.

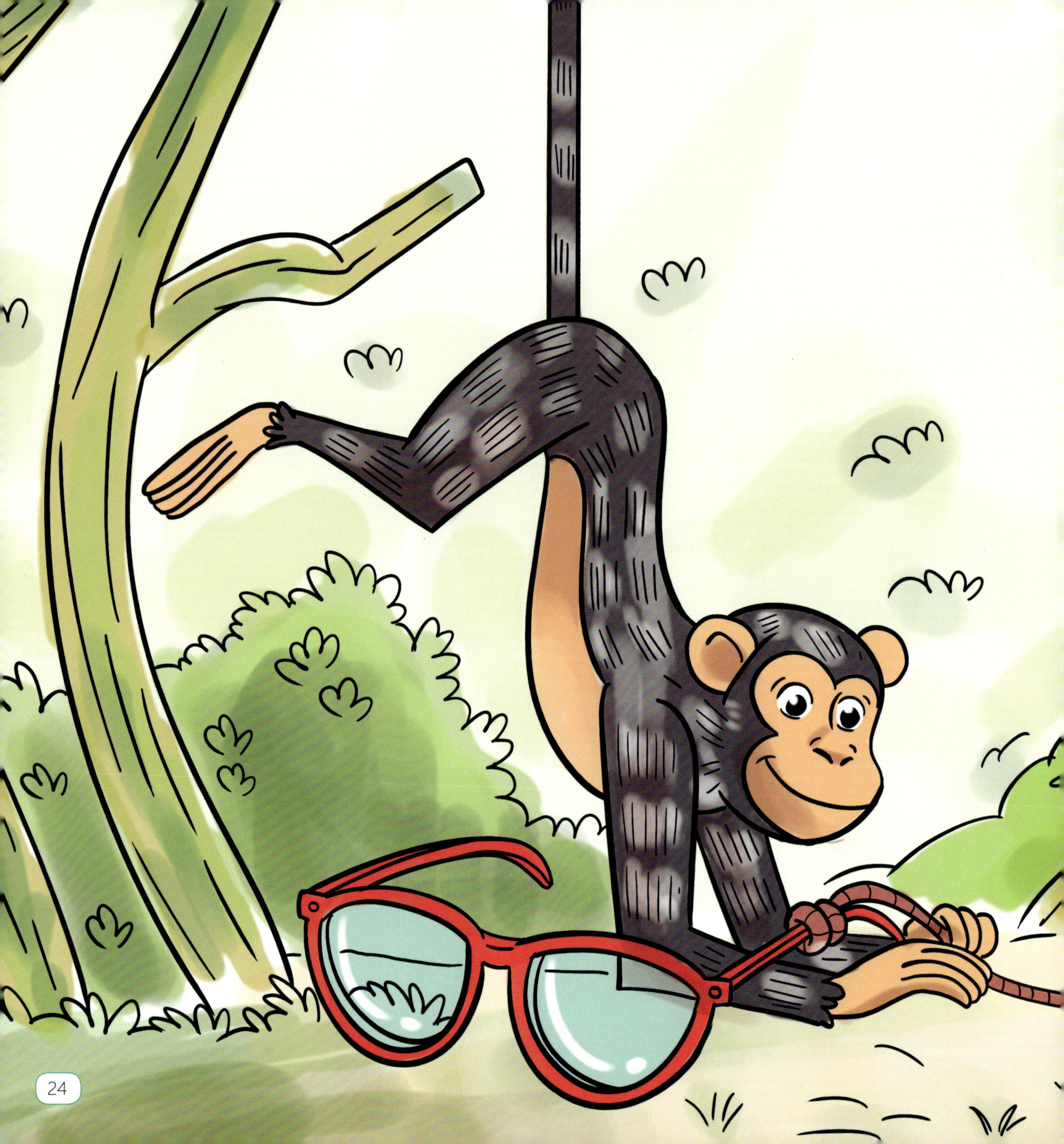

"I know what you're thinking," Donovan said as he raced back down the tree. He was back in a flash with a piece of rope. "I can use this to tie the sunglasses to your tail. That way you can drag them back," Donovan said as he got to work attaching the rope to Anthony's tail.

The next day was Bruno's birthday. Again, Anthony snuck out to the shed. It took a lot of pushing and rolling, but Anthony finally got all the gifts into Bruno's cave.

Bruno woke to find Anthony standing in front of a pile of gifts. "What's all this?" Bruno asked as he loudly yawned. When Bruno yawned it sounded like thunder and a growl all mixed together.

"Happy birthday, Bruno!" Anthony cheered as he raced toward his friend. "Even though you haven't met them, Sophia, Dylan, Grayson and Donovan all wanted to give you a gift to celebrate your special day!"

Anthony was smiling on the outside, but on the inside, he was feeling a bit sad.

"I tried to throw you a party, but you were right. Nobody could find a way to get here. The party was supposed to be my gift to you, and now I don't have anything at all." All his plans had fallen apart. After all that work, he didn't even have a gift for his friend.

Bruno was shocked, not just by the gifts, but by his friend's words.

"Anthony, this is the most amazing thing anyone has ever done for me."

"You're sure you're not disappointed?" Anthony asked quietly.

"I'm positive. Nobody has ever put so much thought and hard work into making my birthday this special."

Bruno was delighted that the other animals at the zoo thought enough of him to give him such wonderful gifts. The flowers smelled nice, the peanuts were salty and crunchy, the ball would be a lot of fun to play with, and his new sunglasses were the perfect fit.

That day, when the guests came to see Bruno for his birthday, they found a giant polar bear wearing bright red sunglasses floating around the pool with a little lizard sleeping on his belly.

THE END

Meet Sophia

- Giraffes are the tallest mammals on Earth. They can grow as tall as 18 feet (that's as tall as a 2-story house)!
- Each giraffe has a unique spot pattern. Just like human fingerprints, no two giraffes have the same spot pattern.
- A giraffe's tongue is 18 inches long and has the ability to grip and wrap around things.
- Giraffes live in families which can be called a troop, kindergarten, or tower.

Meet Dylan

- Bottlenose dolphins live in warm oceans but need to breathe air just like humans! They can hold their breath for up to 10 minutes!
- Dolphins can jump 16 feet out of the water (this is called breaching)!
- They use a series of high-pitched clicks, called echolocation, to find food and communicate.
- 10-20 dolphins live, play and hunt together in groups called pods.

Meet Grayson

- African elephants are the heaviest animals on Earth. They can weigh as much as 14,000 pounds (that's as much as a school bus)!
- Their ears are not just for hearing. Flapping their ears helps them release heat like a built-in air conditioner!
- Their tusks are actually massive teeth!
- They live in groups called herds. Male elephants leave the herd when they are 12-15 years old.
- African elephants can live for 60-70 years.

Meet Donovan

- Spider monkeys live in the rainforest and are about the size of a toddler—2 feet tall and about 25 pounds.
- They tend to hang from trees by their tails which makes them look like a spider!
- Spider monkeys are the only monkeys without an opposable thumb.
- They live in groups called troops and the troop leader is always female.

About the Author & Illustrator

MEGAN DELIBERTO-*AUTHOR*

Megan grew up reading everything she could get her hands on and dreamed of being a children's librarian. She now spends her days visiting schools and libraries throughout the Midwest reading her own stories and helping children fall in love with books. Her first book, No Place for a Lizard, was published in 2022 and has received the gold award for family-friendly media.

Megan lives in the Chicago suburbs with her husband, son, and their pets.

She is still an avid reader and enjoys hiking, watching football and loves all things Star Wars.

Want Megan to visit your school? Please visit www.megandauthor.com to schedule a visit!

Follow Megan on Facebook @MeganDelibertoAuthor,
Instagram @megandauthor and TikTok @megandeliberto03

TIEMOKO SYLLA-*ILLUSTRATOR*

Tiemoko lives in Abidjan, Ivory Coast. He started taking his first illustration commissions as early as the second grade; his classmates requested drawings of human organs among other things!

Since 2017, Tiemoko has been working with Bayard Afrique, which publishes the magazine Planete Jaime Lire. Every month, Tiemoko creates characters, backgrounds and the game pages for the magazine as well as illustrating children's books.

Tiemoko regularly leads workshops and animated storytelling shows.

He is deeply influenced by Morris (Maurice de Bevere). You may further find Tiemoko's work on his Instagram page (tiem_sylla) where he gives a behind the scenes look at his illustrations coming to life.

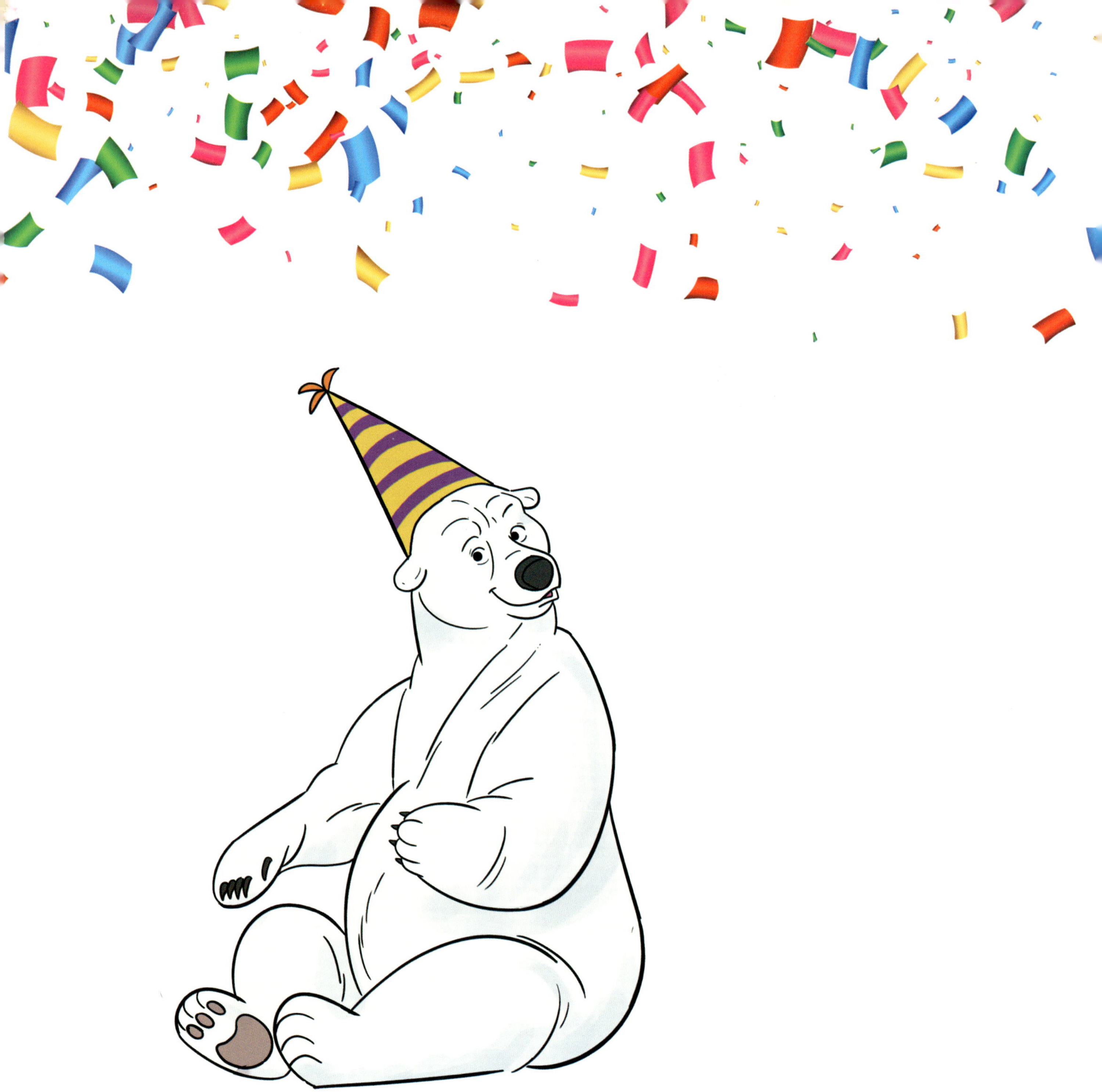